MATHEMATIC MARVELS!

The Math of Nature

Written by Anne Rooney

WORLD BOOK

www.worldbook.com

Co-published by agreement between Shi Tu Hui and World Book, Inc.

Shi Tu Hui
Room 1807, Block 1,
#3 West Dawang Road
Chaoyang District, Beijing 100025
P.R. China

World Book, Inc.
180 North LaSalle Street
Suite 900
Chicago, Illinois 60601
USA

© 2026. All rights reserved. This volume may not be reproduced in whole or in part in any form without prior written permission from the publisher.

WORLD BOOK and the GLOBE DEVICE are registered trademarks or trademarks of World Book, Inc.

Library of Congress Control Number: 2025942224

Aha! Academy: Math
ISBN: 978-0-7166-7377-4 (set, hardcover)

Mathematic Marvels! The Math of Nature
ISBN: 978-0-7166-7381-1 (hard cover)
ISBN: 978-0-7166-7444-3 (e-book)
ISBN: 978-0-7166-7434-4 (soft cover)

Staff

Editorial

Vice President
Tom Evans

Editorial Project Coordinator
Kaile Kilner

Senior Curriculum Designer
Caroline Davidson

Curriculum Designer
Mikayla Kightlinger

Proofreader
Nathalie Strassheim

Indexer
Nathaniel Lindstrom

Graphics and Design

Senior Visual
Communications Designer
Melanie Bender

Designer
Shannon Hagman

Written by Anne Rooney

Designed by Starletta Polster

Acknowledgments

The publishers gratefully acknowledge the following sources for photography. All illustrations were prepared by WORLD BOOK unless otherwise noted.

Cover: K-Shoot Background/Shutterstock; Neale Cousland/Shutterstock; PINA/Shutterstock; PixProfessional/Shutterstock; Vojce/Shutterstock

© IanDagnall Computing/Alamy 38; © Trinity Mirror/Mirrorpix/Alamy 15; © Raphael GAILLARDE/Gamma-Rapho/Getty Images; NASA 22, 33; © Shutterstock 4, 5, 6, 7, 8, 9, 10, 11, 12, 13, 14, 15, 16, 17, 18, 19, 20, 21, 22, 23, 24, 25, 26, 27, 28, 29, 30, 31, 32, 33, 34, 35, 36, 37, 38, 39, 40, 41, 42, 43, 44, 45, 46, 47, 48

There is a glossary of terms on page 48. Terms defined in the glossary are in type that looks like *this* on their first appearance on any spread (two facing pages).

Contents

Introduction 4

1 Seeing shapes 6
    A good fit. 8
    Scutes and shells 10

2 Building bodies 12
    Fold yourself in half 14
    Arms all around! .16
    Special spirals 18

3 Inside and outside .20
    How big can you be? 22
    Fat and thin 24
    Fancy surfaces 26

4 Frilly fractals 28
    Root and branch .30
    Endless edges 32

5 Survive! 34
    How many babies? 36
    Growing populations. 38
    Prime time 40
    Ten percent dinner 42

Create a creature! 44
Index 46
Glossary 48

Introduction

When you walk in a forest or along a beach, when you watch snow fall or collect pine cones, you probably aren't thinking about math. But math is all around you in nature—in the shapes, numbers, arrangements, and sequences of natural objects and living things.

You can find math in the shapes of animals and plants, in the ways animals build their homes, and when and how they have their babies. It's in the wiggles of the coastline and the curves of a shell. You can't get away from math!

My shell is beautiful and *mathematical!*

SEEING SHAPES

The natural world is full of shapes, but few of them are the perfect *geometrical* figures you come across in a math lesson! If you go into a forest or a meadow, you won't see many perfect squares. No animal is triangular, and few are perfectly circular. You will see lots of curves, including rough circles and *spirals*, and lots of branching lines.

Take a look around the natural world and you'll be sure to find lines, curves, and angles. Read on to discover more about elements of shapes in nature.

A Baya weaver bird builds a nest with a hole at the bottom to make it difficult for **predators** to get in—it can only be accessed from the air!

The math of shapes is important in nature. All plants and animals need to work over flat areas and move through volumes. They have area and volume themselves. They might have a body covered with scales that fit together, or build a home that is a special shape. Let's look at how some shapes work with math in nature!

A snake's scales must fit together perfectly. They overlap, making a smooth surface.

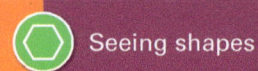
Seeing shapes

A good fit

Three simple, regular shapes tesselate perfectly, leaving no gaps: *hexagons,* squares, and *equilateral triangles.*

Bees build honeycomb from *hexagonal* cells made of wax. They store their honey in these cells. By making all the cells the same size and shape, bees can build up a honeycomb starting from different places and know it will all fit together.

Have you noticed that some shapes fit together well when repeated, leaving no gaps between them? These shapes *tesselate*. You can see them in paving and tiling, but they happen in nature, too.

Diamond-shaped fish scales tesselate.

It costs bees work and resources to make wax for their honeycomb. They don't want to waste any. It turns out that hexagons are the most efficient shape for them to use, taking the least wax to make the most storage space. Math helps bees save energy, resources, and space, storing their honey as efficiently as possible.

The Roman writer **Marcus Terentius Varro** suggested more than 2,000 years ago that hexagons can store more honey for the same amount of wax than other shapes. In 1999, mathematician Thomas Hales proved him right.

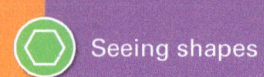
Seeing shapes

Scutes and shells

Lots of animals have compound eyes, which are eyes are made of lots of tiny separate sections side by side. A dragonfly eye has 28,000 tiny hexagonal lenses arranged like an upturned dish.

Turtles and tortoises have a shell made of panels called scutes that fit together. These are not all the same shape. As the turtle grows, each scute gets bigger from the edges. The pattern stays the same.

This turtle's shell has irregular **hexagons** in a central row, surrounded by pentagons (five-sided shapes) on each side. Then the whole shell is edged with rectangles.

Honeycomb is flat, but some tessellations cover curved surfaces. These often use more than one shape. We can find lots of examples in nature—let's take a look!

Lots of tessellations in nature are irregular. The shapes fit together perfectly, but are all different. You can find them in the wings of a dragonfly, the coat of a giraffe, and the cells of onion skin. With a magnifying glass, you can even see tessellations on your own skin!

Onion skin cells

TECH TIME

A miniature camera copying an insect's compound eye has been developed for use in medicine. The tiny cameras with lenses arranged in a *hemisphere* can be threaded inside a patient's body to get a clear, wide-angle view.

2 BUILDING BODIES

Paired wings enable the owl to fly. If one wing was bigger than the other, it couldn't fly properly.

An owl swoops from the sky on paired wings, snatching a mouse with the talons of its two feet and flying off to eat its meal. It has only one tail and one beak, though. How much harder it would be if its wings were different sizes, one foot was in front of the other, and the beak was on the side of its head?! The shape and structure of animal bodies are perfectly suited to the ways they live their lives.

Once you start to see shapes in nature, it becomes easier to spot patterns created by those shapes. What repetitions do you notice?

The shells of sea urchins are built from similar segments organized around a central point.

One way animal bodies are structured to help them is through *symmetry*. This is how identical parts of the animal are positioned. Animals can be symmetrical in different ways—and sometimes not at all. Plants often don't seem to have a *regular shape*, but even they are structured to work well in their environment.

Eyes at the front of an owl's head give it keen vision with good *depth perception*, meaning it can judge distances well. Their identical placing on either side of the beak means it see can straight forward and equally to the right and left of its body.

Right monocular vision

Binocular vision

Left monocular vison

70 degrees

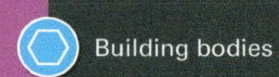 Building bodies

Fold yourself in half

In math, a figure is reflected if it's a mirror image of its original. A reflected figure matches the original if you flip one over, then they fit with no overlap.

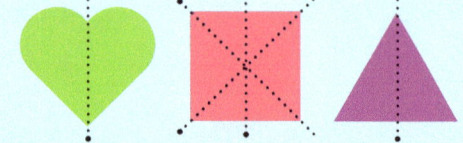

Animals have reflected symmetry because they develop as embryos on two sides of a central line, which is their *axis of symmetry*. Yours is your backbone. Symmetry gives you two arms, two legs, two eyes, and a single, centrally placed nose. But you have only one heart, and it's not in the middle!

Can you believe that most animals are symmetrical? It's true! Even the human body is symmetrical. If you could fold yourself in half along your backbone, your left and right sides would fit over each other almost perfectly! This is called reflective (or bilateral) *symmetry*.

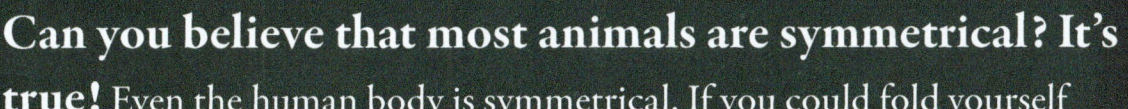

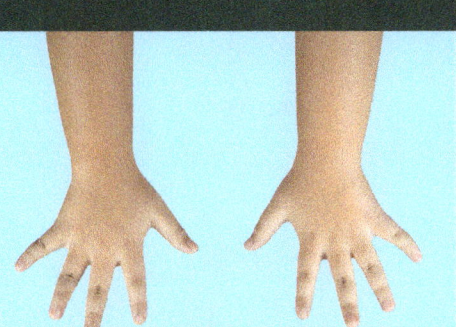

Your hands are mirror images of each other. This makes them much more useful than if you had two hands with a thumb on the left, say. Some single body parts are also symmetrical. Each vertebra in your backbone is symmetrical and so is your brain.

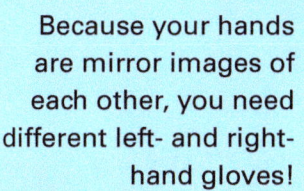

Because your hands are mirror images of each other, you need different left- and right-hand gloves!

CURIOUS CONNECTIONS

PSYCHOLOGY

Psychologists say we find people most attractive if they have very symmetrical faces. They suggest this is because it signals the person developed well in the womb and so makes a good mate for producing healthy babies.

Building bodies

Arms all around!

Starfish have five or more arms. Each arm looks the same. The animal has rotational *symmetry* because you can make its shape by taking an arm and part of the central body and rotating it.

A starfish with five parts has order 5 symmetry. This means that if it is rotated in a full circle, it makes a shape with five identical sections.

Many flowers, and some entire plants, have rotational symmetry. A daisy with 23 petals has order 23 symmetry.

Not all organisms can be folded in half! An animal like a sea urchin has *radial* or *rotational symmetr*y: their body pattern can be made by rotating part of their body around a central point.

A structure like a round pollen grain looks the same however you turn it. These structures have spherical symmetry.

Other organisms are not symmetrical at all. Some types of sponge or fungus grow into odd, blobby shapes. They don't have separate organs inside and don't need to be symmetrical.

DID YOU KNOW?

If a starfish arm is detached with a bit of the middle part, it can grow to be a whole new starfish!

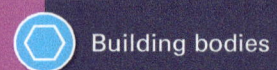

Building bodies

Special spirals

Some plants grow leaves in symmetrical pairs one above another, while others grow them singly or in pairs rotated by a fraction of a turn. The leaves come from the stem in a *spiral* at regular angles. Plants gather sunlight with their leaves. A plant that grows leaves in a spiral prevents its upper leaves shading lower leaves, so it gains as much light as it can.

CAREER CORNER

Meteorologists study how storms and hurricanes form—and even storms on other planets, such as the gas giant Jupiter. The rotation of the planet makes the winds, which otherwise blow in a straight line, twist into a spiral. Meteorologists calculate the wind speeds and how quickly the storm is moving to warn people of coming danger.

If you look closely at a plant, you will find there is a pattern to how the leaves grow from the stem. But these patterns show up in other areas of nature, too!

Nature contains many spirals, from snail shells to galaxies, and they are usually *logarithmic* spirals. In a normal (arithmetic) spiral, the lines remain the same distance apart. In a logarithmic spiral, the lines get farther apart moving away from the center. Logarithmic spirals appear in the arrangement of seeds and petals, the shapes of spiral galaxies, and the shells of some mollusks.

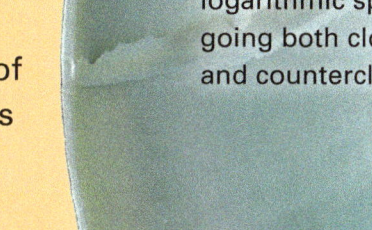

The seeds on a sunflower head are arranged in logarithmic spirals going both clockwise and counterclockwise.

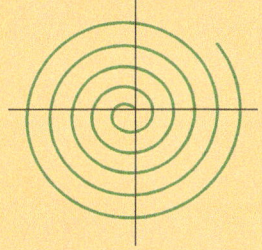

Archimedean (arithmetic) spiral

Logarithmic spiral

A snail shell grows with the snail. As the snail gets bigger, the last spiral of its shell needs to be larger so it can fit inside. That's why it has to grow in a logarithmic spiral.

It's easy to see this chunky snail couldn't fit in its shell if the spiral stayed the same width as the central turns!

3
INSIDE AND OUTSIDE

Area, perimeter, and volume all play important roles in the world's natural processes. These mathematical concepts help us understand the shapes, sizes, and spaces that make up our environment. Let's explore how math helps shape our world!

Have you ever noticed how a thin pancake gets cold much more quickly than a chunky baked potato? The pancake has a lot of outside (surface area) compared to its inside (volume), while the potato has less outside for the amount of inside.

Lots of surface area!

Lots of volume!

The amount of space an object occupies in three dimensions is called its volume. It's measured in three directions.

A lily pad has a large area, but is very thin. Its surface area (the total area of its surfaces) is large compared to its small volume. The frog is chunky: It has a large volume compared to its surface area.

20

Area is measured in two directions. The size of a rug or a garden is given as its area. An area doesn't need to be flat. Any surface has an area, even if it's wrapped around something. An adult human has about 22 square feet of skin!

The outline of a shape is its perimeter. Some shapes have a large perimeter for a small area. Circles have the smallest possible perimeter for the area they enclose.

By standing in a circle, prey animals reduce the number of individuals around the edges (perimeter) of the group that could be caught by hungry hunters.

In nature, the relationships between volume, area, and perimeter are very important. Many processes take place at surfaces or edges. Read on to discover how the volume, surface area, and perimeters of plants and animals suit how they live!

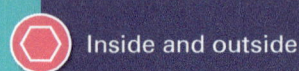

Inside and outside

How big can you be?

Whales are very heavy. A blue whale weighs around 300,000 pounds. In the ocean, water supports its weight as it swims. But on land, a whale would need legs. They would have to be very thick and strong to support such a heavy body.

Sauropod dinosaurs grew to huge sizes, but they were nowhere near as heavy as a whale.

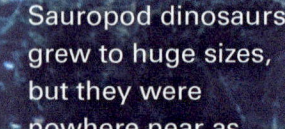

CAREER CORNER

Engineers designing spacecraft have to balance the size of a rocket with the amount of fuel it needs to leave Earth. The bigger the rocket, the more fuel it needs, so then it has to be even bigger—and then it needs even more fuel!

Blue whales are the largest animals on Earth. They live in the sea; could a whale evolve to live on land? Almost certainly not—math won't let it!

Imagine we super-sized an elephant, doubling its size in all directions: twice as high, twice as long, twice as wide. Its volume—and so its weight—would increase by **2 × 2 × 2 = 8.**

But a *cross-section* of (slice through) its bones and muscles would only increase by a factor of **4 (2 × 2)**, so they would be too weak to support its heavy body. The elephant would need to get much stronger, thicker legs. And then it would be even heavier. That's why we don't have giant elephants or land-going whales.

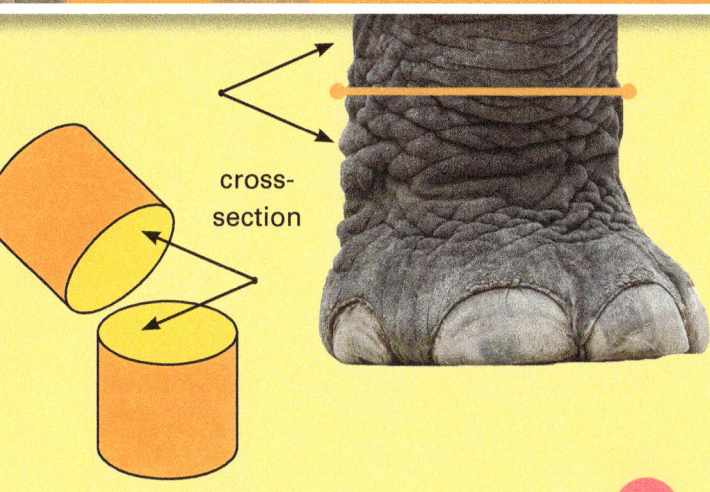

cross-section

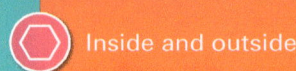
Inside and outside

Fat and thin

A cube of clay with a volume of 1 cubic inch has six faces, each with an area of (1 × 1) = 1 square inch. Its surface area is 6 square inches. Mathematicians call the relationship between surface area to volume a *ratio*. The surface-area-to-volume ratio of this cube is written 6:1. The ratio lets you compare two quantities.

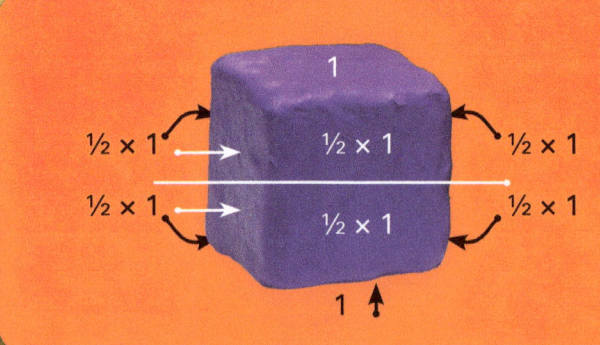

If you cut the cube in half, each half has two faces of 1 square inch and four surfaces of (½ × 1) = ½ square inch, totalling 4 square inches. The total surface area of both halves is 8 square inches, but the volume is still 1 cubic inch. The surface-area-to-volume ratio is now 8:1.

10 slices

If you cut the cube into 10 thin slices, the surface-area-to-volume ratio is 24:1.

If you've ever used modeling clay, you will have noticed that you can make more thin things than fat things with the same amount of clay. The same idea is true in nature: Animals and plants use their shapes to maximize or minimize surface area for different purposes.

Anything that happens at a surface happens more quickly as the surface-area-to-volume ratio increases. A leaf needs a lot of surface area to absorb lots of sunlight, so a high surface-area-to-volume ratio is usually good. A small animal loses heat over its body surface. Many small animals sleep curled into a ball to reduce their surface-area-to-volume ratio, which mean less area is exposed to the cold air.

A dormouse sleeps curled into a ball to get the smallest surface area for its volume, helping it stay warm.

The fat body of a cactus has a low surface-area-to-volume ratio, so it doesn't lose water too fast.

Leaves take in the energy of sunlight over their surface. A leaf is thin, with a large area. It takes in as much sunlight as possible for the leaf-material the tree has grown.

Inside and outside

Fancy surfaces

The small intestine (part of your gut) is lined with villi, which look like tiny fingers sticking out of the surface. These absorb *nutrients* from your food. The more surface area your gut has, the more nutrients it can absorb.

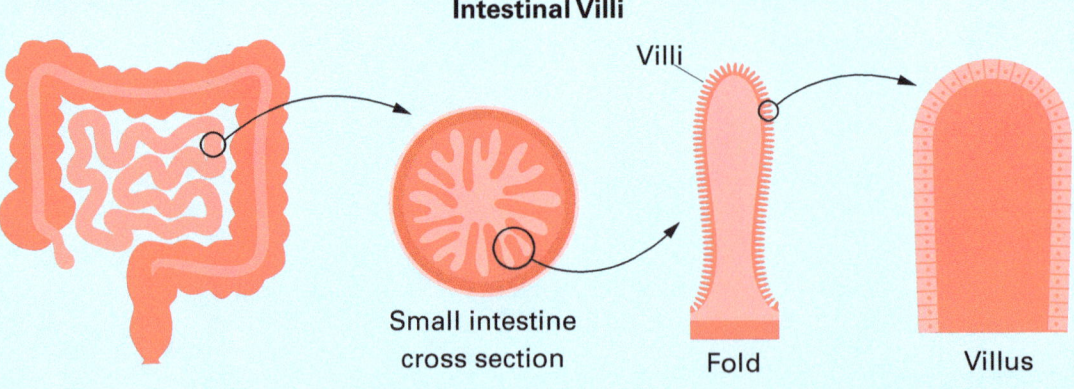

Intestinal Villi

Small intestine cross section

Villi

Fold

Villus

Your intestines are a very long, thin tube folded and curled inside you. Imagine taking 15 feet of string and screwing it up in your hand—although it's long, it fits easily in your fist. Your intestine is just as long (but thicker, at about an inch across). With its folds, wrinkles, and villi, the area for digesting food is about 200 times the area of your skin—all squashed up inside you!

Lots of things in nature are frilly, bumpy, or wrinkly. This is one of Nature's tricks for increasing surface area. Anywhere that you see frills, bumps, wrinkles, or bobbles, look for something that happens at the surface!

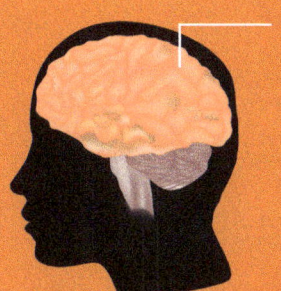
Wrinkled human brain

Smooth fish brain

Surfaces are crucial. Thinking happens at the surface of the brain, so with a wrinklier brain, you can do more mental work. A fish's brain is much smoother than yours.

The airways in your lungs split up into many branches, each ending with a tiny sack-shape where oxygen passes into your blood. The surface area inside an adult's lungs is over 120 square feet (70 square meters)!

CURIOUS CONNECTIONS

CHEMISTRY In chemistry—or cooking—breaking something into small pieces helps it to dissolve more quickly. A large lump of salt will dissolve much more slowly than the same volume of ground salt because the ground salt has much more surface area in contact with the water.

FRILLY FRACTALS

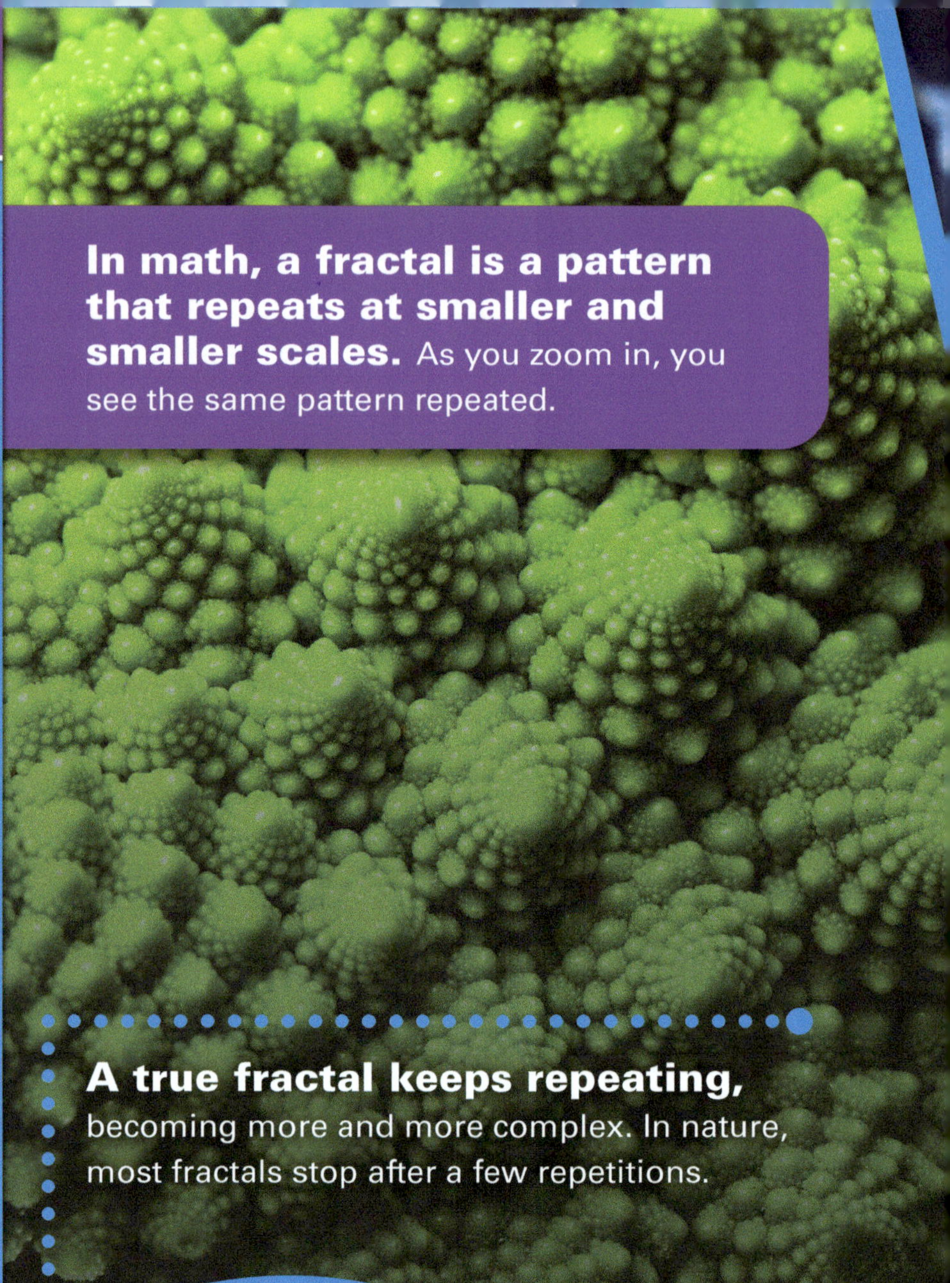

In math, a fractal is a pattern that repeats at smaller and smaller scales. As you zoom in, you see the same pattern repeated.

A true fractal keeps repeating, becoming more and more complex. In nature, most fractals stop after a few repetitions.

Have you ever noticed how branching trees, lightning, and blood vessels all look similar? All have a thick stem breaking into smaller and smaller branches. They're examples of *fractals* in nature.

Polish mathematician **Benoit Mandelbrot** was the first person to draw fractal sets using a computer. He showed how complex patterns can be made from a simple mathematical rule, and that many chaotic-looking natural shapes follow a pattern.

A Mandelbrot set creates a shape with an outline that looks increasingly intricate the more closely you zoom in.

A fractal can be a system of lines or an enclosed shape. There are hidden fractals all around us in the natural world—let's go and spot some!

Frilly fractals

Root and branch

Take a tree branch. It splits into two, and then the two smaller branches also split the same way, and so on, down to the smallest twigs. And it's not just huge trees—many smaller plants do the same. A single floret of broccoli has the same structure as the whole head of broccoli.

The veins in a leaf split and split again, making a network that covers the surface of the leaf.

Branch once Branch twice Branch three times

Trees, lungs, blood vessels, lightning, rivers… they all share a pattern of branching and dividing. It's a type of fractal that appears throughout nature.

Fractals work in such structures as lungs and root systems to make a network that packs in lots of surface area. Roots penetrate the soil with many tiny rootlets that can take in water all over their surface. Blood vessels break into ever smaller branches to deliver blood to all parts of your body.

CURIOUS CONNECTIONS

ART — Some artists use the self-repeating patterns of fractals in their work. The American painter Jackson Pollock produced large canvases by spattering paint which produced fractal patterns as it fell. He perfected his technique to achieve a high level of fractal geometry.

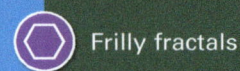
Frilly fractals

Endless edges

The closer you look at a fractal *perimeter*, the longer it gets. In math, a shape with a truly fractal outline has a limited area, but the perimeter can become endless! In nature nothing really has an endless outline, but it can become very difficult to measure.

Snowflakes are not only unique but also fractal. Each "branch" of a snowflake has smaller branches coming off it, those have even smaller branches, and so on. The way snowflakes form is a result of how ice crystals grow. The closer you look, the more intricate their shape appears. But however long the outline grows, the area of the snowflake remains tiny.

Fractals aren't only pathways for carrying water, blood, or air. Some fractals enclose an area, forming the outline or boundary (perimeter) of a shape.

The jagged edge of a coastline remains uneven however closely you look, down to individual pebbles and grains of sand! Rocky shores always become fractal eventually. As pounding waves break off chunks of rock, the changed shape reduces the impact of the waves striking it. A wiggly coastline damps the force of the waves so they can't erode it further.

DID YOU KNOW?

You can draw your own fractal from *equilateral triangles*. The area will always be smaller than that of a circle drawn around the first star, but the perimeter gets steadily longer. This is called a Koch snowflake.

SURVIVE!

5

Do you have any brothers or sisters? Just think how different your life would be if you had a thousand brothers and sisters! Some animals have just a few babies and some have hundreds or even thousands. Yet the world isn't flooded with animals of those types. Math and Nature work together to control the populations of different animals and plants.

For some animals, survival is tied to the math of another species. Pandas eat only bamboo, but bamboo flowers and dies on a cycle of 20 to 60 years. When the bamboo dies, pandas can starve. They need to live in areas with different species of bamboo that flower in different years.

There are math patterns in the lives of living things, in how they reproduce (make young) and how they feed and live. Who knew animals used math?

Survival is a numbers game. Animals need enough food, enough living space, and to have enough babies for their population to continue.

Even us cubs are affected by math!

Survive!

How many babies?

For animal populations to stay the same, each pair must produce two offspring that survive to reproduce. They balance risks, *probabilities*, and family size to make it work.

Large mammals, such as whales, elephants, and humans, usually have only one baby at a time and a small number in total. They care for their babies as they develop, giving them a good chance of survival.

Some animals produce lots of eggs or babies but do not look after them. Many eggs will be eaten or never hatch, and few babies will live to adulthood. If an eel lays 1,000 eggs, it only needs 1 in 500 to survive and breed for the eel population to stay the same.

A human family often has two or three children. A cat might have four, five, or six kittens in a litter—and several litters over a lifetime. Meanwhile, frogs can produce between 3,000 and 20,000 eggs at a time! Yet the world is not knee deep in frogs and there is no plague of kittens.

Plants produce thousands of seeds. Many fall on places they can't grow, some grow but soon die, perhaps being eaten. It seems wasteful, but seedlings that don't survive feed other organisms and help keep an ecosystem going.

Reedmace, or bulrush, scatters thousands of seeds.

Survive!

Growing populations

The Italian mathematician Leonardo Fibonacci wondered how quickly the population of rabbits would grow starting with a single pair. He assumed a rabbit could reproduce after two months and each pair would have a male and female baby each month. No rabbits would die.

Fibonacci found this sequence for the number of pairs of rabbits at the end of each month:

1, 1, 2, 3, 5, 8, 13, 21...

You can continue the sequence by adding the last two numbers together each time:

1 + 1 = 2; 1 + 2 = 3; 2 + 3 = 5; 3 + 5 = 8; 5 + 8 = 13; 8 + 13 = 21; 13 + 21 = 34; 21 + 34 = 55

1

1

2

3

5

8

Rabbits are well known for the number of offspring they can produce. If you look closely and think like a mathematician, you can spot a pattern!

Fibonacci numbers turn up a lot in nature. Many flowers have a Fibonacci-number of petals, for instance. Even though it's called the Fibonacci sequence, it was first described in India by Acharya Pingala around 200 B.C.

Aphids are tiny insects that often reproduce by cloning. Each female can produce around 100 babies—all of which are female and can produce their own babies after just a week. In perfect conditions, and if all the babies survived, one female aphid could lead to 600 billion more in one season!

DID YOU KNOW?

November 23 is known as Fibonacci Day because the date is 1 1 2 3—the first four numbers of the Fibonacci sequence.

Survive!

Prime time

Prime numbers are numbers that can't be divided by any number except themselves and 1.

Examples of prime numbers are:

1, 2, 3, 5, 7, 11, 13, 17, 19, 23, 29, 31.

Apart from 2, all prime numbers are odd. You wouldn't think these would be useful in nature, but they are.

TECH TIME

Prime numbers are used in encryption (making a secret code) for sending data safely across the internet. Computer systems multiply two large prime numbers together to give a much larger number. It's almost impossible for another computer to discover the original numbers. It could work for longer than the universe has been in existence and still not find the answer!

7,153,967,453 × 3,969,854,407 = 28,400,209,220,826,615,371

The world isn't flooded with aphids or tadpoles because so many are eaten. But if too many are eaten, a species doesn't survive. Some animals use a crafty math trick to cheat hungry *predators*.

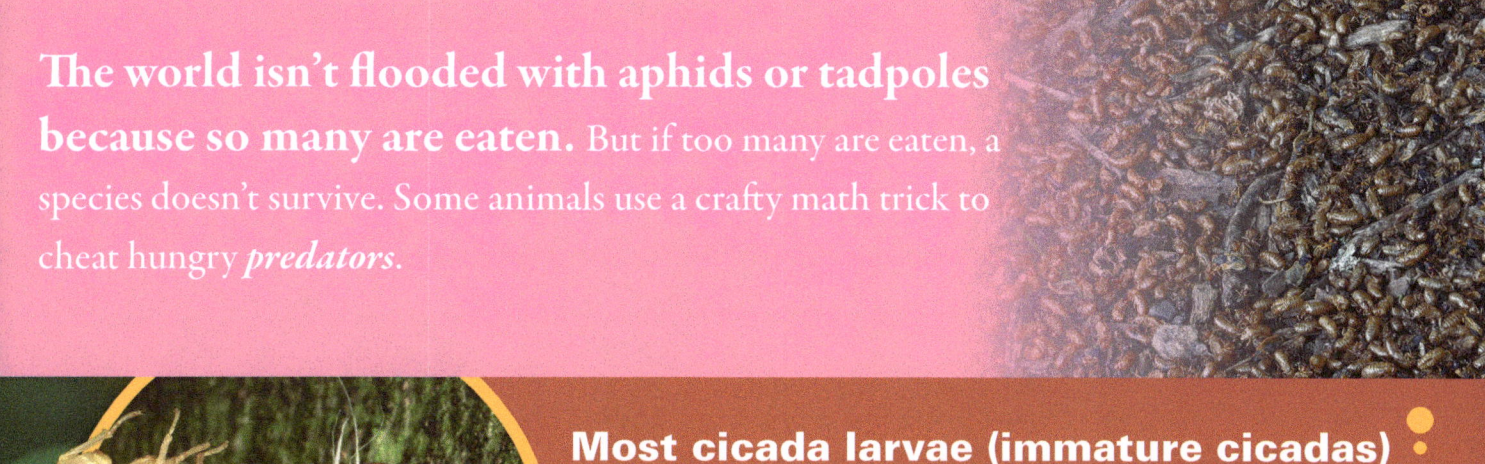

Most cicada larvae (immature cicadas) hide underground in winter and come out in early summer to live as adults and breed. But some types of cicada hide underground for either 13 or 17 years before emerging. Both 13 and 17 are prime numbers. It's a life-saving tactic.

This 17-year periodical cicada is emerging from its nymph case after a long wait underground.

Cicadas make a tasty snack for lots of other animals. By all emerging at once after a long interval, they make sure there are too many for them all to be eaten. Nothing will wait 13 years for its dinner, so nothing will evolve to rely on eating 13-year cicadas. Staying hidden for a prime number of years, the cicada rules out being eaten by an animal that works to a two-year cycle, a three-year cycle, or any other regular cycle.

Bird eating a cicada

 Survive!

Ten percent dinner

Animals gain the energy they need to live from their food. Scientists construct pyramids of energy use that show how food energy moves between living things.

At the bottom of every pyramid are plants or *microbes* that use energy from sunlight, and chemicals from water and the air.

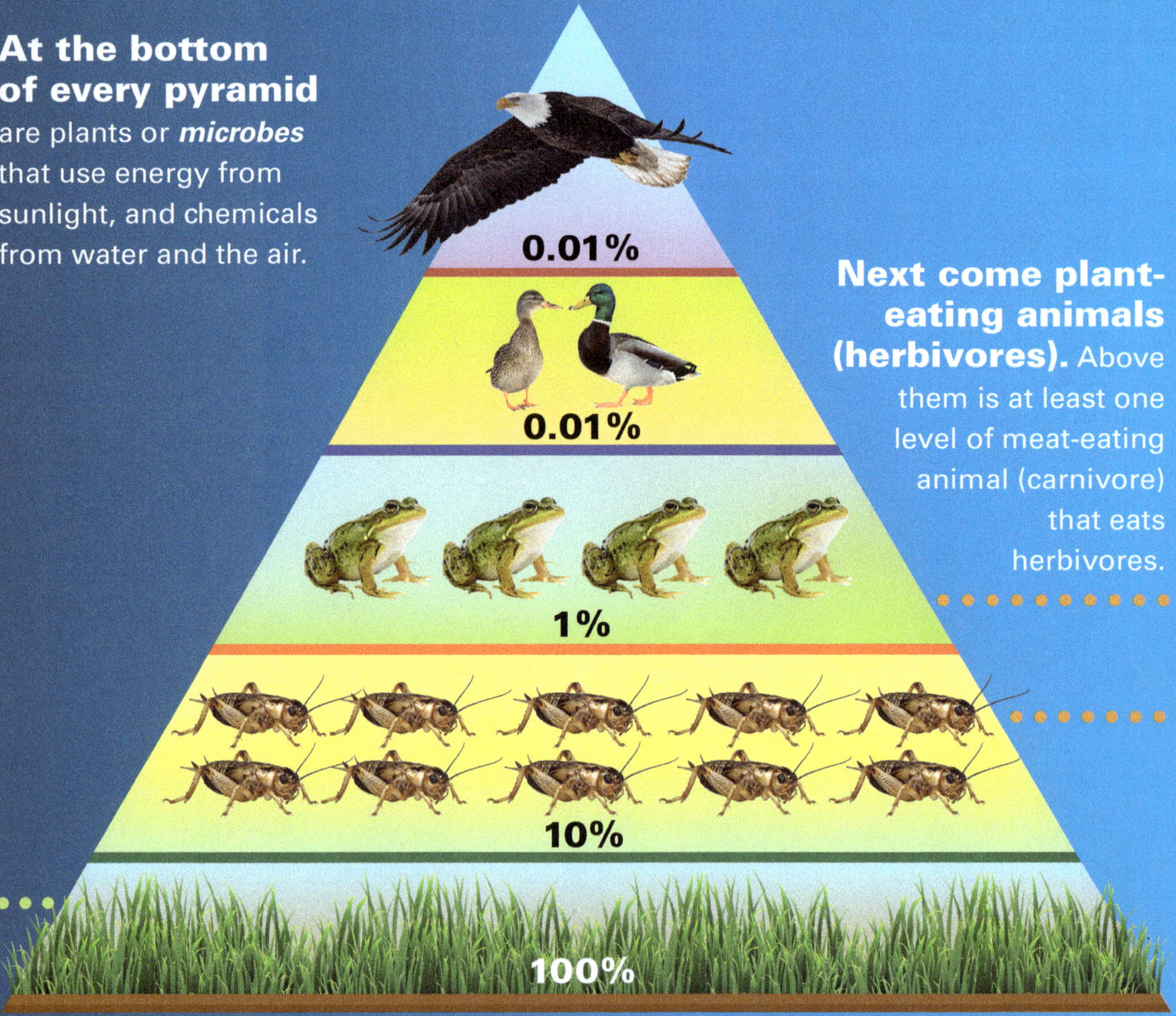

0.01%

0.01%

1%

10%

100%

Next come plant-eating animals (herbivores). Above them is at least one level of meat-eating animal (carnivore) that eats herbivores.

All animals need to eat. Some eat plants, and some eat other animals, or animal products like eggs. This even applies to you: donuts are made of plants (wheat, sugar cane) and animal products (butter from cow milk and eggs from chickens).

CAREER CORNER

Engineers work to make the most of all energy put into a system. They try to make vehicles fuel efficient, buildings efficient in how they use their heating, and solar power generation as productive as possible. Often, energy escapes are heat or in other forms. The aim is to cut these losses to produced energy-efficient systems.

An animal can't use all the energy it gains from food to grow. It also uses energy to stay alive—moving, breathing, running, breeding, and repairing its body. Energy is lost as heat, and when an organism dies but isn't eaten. Only 10 percent of the energy taken is passed up to the next level.

Many solar panels are only 20-25% efficient, meaning 75% of the energy from sunlight falling on them is not converted to electricity. Improving efficiency will help the world to transition to renewable energy.

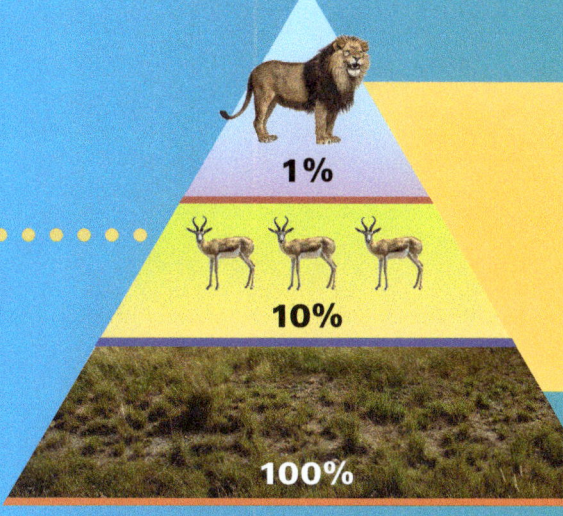

This 10 percent rule limits how many levels there can be. Very few energy pyramids have more than five levels. The numbers just don't add up for more eaters!

Create a creature!

You will need:
- Paper
- Pencil, eraser
- Colored pencils or pens

Give it a try

1. Decide on the type of animal you want to design. Where will it live? What will it eat? What challenges does it face in its life? For example, will it need to keep warm or cool? Does it live somewhere dry or wet? Does it need to save water or stay dry?
2. Draw a picture of your new organism. Think carefully about what its body looks like:
   a. Does it have patterns or shapes that fit together?
   b. What type of symmetry does it have?
   c. Does it have a large or small surface-area-to-volume ratio?

Plants and animals that survive have evolved to be well suited to their environment. They can find food, stay the right temperature, find or make somewhere to live, have their young, and escape from *predators*. In this activity, you will have the chance to think about all of these and design your own animal, using the natural math tricks you have learned in the book.

3. Add labels and text blocks to show how math helps your organism survive. Think about your organism and how math helps it survive. Write down the following on the same sheet of paper you drew it on:
   a. How many babies it has and how many survive
   b. How it gains food; draw an energy pyramid for it
   c. How the shape of its body and insides helps it to survive

Try this next!

Next time you're outside, take some time to observe the world around you. What examples of math do you see in the nature where you live?

How does math affect living things in nature?

Index

A
aphids, 39
arithmetic spirals, 18
art, 31
axis of symmetry, 14

B
bamboo, 35
Baya weaver birds, 7
bees, 8-9
bilateral symmetry. *See* reflective symmetry
brains, 15, 27

C
cacti, 25
cameras, 11
chemistry, 27
cicadas, 40-41
coastlines, 33
compound eyes, 10-11

D
depth perception, 13
dinosaurs, 23
dragonflies, 10-11

E
encryption, 41
energy pyramids, 42-43
engineering (career), 23, 43
equilateral triangles, 8, 33

F
Fibonacci numbers, 38-39
flowers, 15, 18, 39
fractals, 28-33

G
galaxies, 18

H
Hales, Thomas, 9
hemispheres, 11
hexagons, 8-10
honeycomb, 8-9, 11

I
intestines, 26
irregular shapes, 10-11

K
Koch snowflakes, 33

L
logarithmic spirals, 18-19
lungs, 27, 31

M
Mandelbrot sets, 29
meteorology (career), 19
microbes, 42

N
nutrients, 26

O
owls, 12-13

P
pandas, 35
perimeter, 20-21, 32-33
Pingala, Acharya, 39
Pollock, Jackson, 31
predators, 7, 41, 45
prime numbers, 40-41
probability, 36
psychology, 15

R
rabbits, 38-39
radial symmetry. *See* rotational symmetry
ratios, 24-25
reflective symmetry, 14-15
regular shapes, 8
reproduction, 34-39
rotational symmetry, 16-17

S
scales, 7, 9
scutes, 10
sea urchins, 13, 17
shells, 10, 13, 18-19
snails, 18-19
snakes, 7
snowflakes, 32
spherical symmetry, 17
spirals, 6, 18-19
starfish, 16-17
surface area, 20-21, 24-27, 31
symmetry, 13-18

T
tessellation, 8-9, 11
turtles, 10

V
Varro, Marcus Terentius, 9
villi, 26
volume, 7, 20-22, 24-25, 27, 31

W
whales, 22-23, 36

Glossary

axis of symmetry (AK sihs ov SIHM uh tree)—line around which a shape or object is symmetrical

bulbous (BUHL bus)—with a fat, rounded shape

depth perception (dehpth puhr SEHP shuhn)—the ability to see distances, judging which objects are near and which are far way

equilateral triangle (EE kwuh LAT uhr uhl TRY ANG guhl)—a triangle with all sides the same length

geometrical (JEE uh MEHT ruh kuhl)—relating to shapes and their mathematical properties

hemisphere (HEHM uh sfihr)—half of a sphere

hexagon (HEHK suh gon)—a closed shape with six straight sides of the same length

irregular shape (ih REHG yuh luhr shayp)—a shape that does not have a regular pattern of side lengths and angles between the sides

meteorologist (MEE tee uh ROL uh jihst)—a person who works on weather and the climate

microbe (MY krohb)—a living thing too small to see without a microscope (also called microorganism)

nutrient (NOO tree uhnt)—chemical essential for life, to build, repair and operate bodies; animals gain nutrients from food

perimeter (puh RIHM uh tuhr)—the outline or boundary of a shape

predator (PREHD uh tuhr)—an animal that hunts or attacks other animals to eat them

probabilities (PROB uh BIHL uh tee)—the chances of events happening

psychologist (sy KOL uh jihst)—a person who works on the structure, nature, and functioning of the brain

ratio (RAY shee oh)—comparison in terms of size of two numbers

regular shape (REHG yuh luhr shayp)—a shape that has sides and angles in a set relationship to each other, such as a square, hexagon or triangle

spiral (SPY ruhl)—line that follows a circular pattern around a point, but moving ever farther away from the point at the center

symmetry (SIHM uh tree)—the condition of having identical parts, either facing each other or arranged around a central point

tesselate (teh suh layt)—to make a pattern of interlocking shapes leaving no spaces or overlaps

www.ingramcontent.com/pod-product-compliance
Lightning Source LLC
Chambersburg PA
CBHW061252170426
43191CB00041B/2416